5

I Wish Daddy Didn't Drink So Much

I Wish Daddy Didn't Drink So Much

Story and pictures by Judith Vigna

Albert Whitman & Company
Niles, Illinois

OTHER BOOKS BY JUDITH VIGNA

Anyhow, I'm Glad I Tried
Couldn't We Have a Turtle Instead?
Daddy's New Baby
Everyone Goes as a Pumpkin
Grandma Without Me
Gregorio Y Sus Puntos
Gregory's Stitches
The Hiding House
The Little Boy Who Loved Dirt and
Almost Became a Superslob
Mommy and Me by Ourselves Again
Nobody Wants a Nuclear War
She's Not My Real Mother

Library of Congress Cataloging-in-Publication Data

Vigna, Judith.
  I wish Daddy didn't drink so much / story and pictures by Judith
Vigna.
      p. cm.
    Summary: After a disappointing Christmas, Lisa learns ways to deal
with her father's alcoholism with the help of her mother and an
older friend.
  ISBN 0-8075-3523-0
 [1. Alcoholism—Fiction. 2. Fathers—Fiction.] I. Title.
PZ7.V67Iab 1988
[E]—dc19
                              88-108
                               CIP
                               AC

Text and illustrations © 1988 by Judith Vigna
Published in 1988 by Albert Whitman & Company, Niles, Illinois
Published simultaneously in Canada by General Publishing, Limited, Toronto
All rights reserved. Printed in the United States of America.
10 9 8 7 6 5 4 3 2 1

For N., who is winning the battle.

For Christmas, Daddy made me a sled. He brought it to my room on Christmas Eve. I knew it was only Daddy in a Santa Claus suit because he bumped into my bed twice and spilled beer on the rug. I didn't like that. When Daddy drinks a lot of beer, he acts funny.

But I loved that he built me a sled. It was shiny
blue with little stenciled flowers. There was a note
that said:

Dear Lisa,
   Your dad promised me
he'll take you sledding
right after breakfast.
         Love,
         Santa

I knew it wasn't really Santa's writing, but I
didn't care. Daddy and I haven't had any fun in a
long time.

After breakfast, Daddy didn't want to go
sledding. "Later," he growled. He didn't even look
at the Christmas card I drew. I made it in school,
especially for him. I helped Mommy fix the turkey.
She had bought an extra big one because her new
friend, Mrs. Field, was coming for Christmas
dinner. They met at a meeting for people who have
a lot of drinking in their family.

Mommy says it's okay to talk to Mrs. Field about
Daddy's drinking. Before, I wasn't allowed to tell
anyone.

While the turkey was cooking, I asked Daddy, "Can we go sledding now?"

"Later," he said.

I got mad. "But you *promised!*"

"Don't bug me!" he shouted. "Get lost!"

I hate when Daddy yells at me. I'm scared he'll hit me. I stayed quiet and played with my new toys. I pretended my sled could fly, just like Santa's, over the clouds to a warm place.

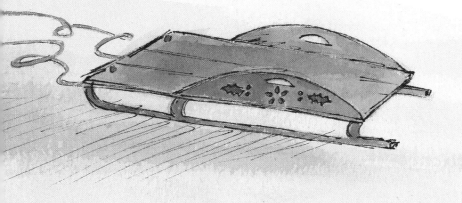

When it was time to set the table, I put out an extra plate, but Mommy took it away.

"Isn't Mrs. Field eating with us?" I asked.

"No," Mommy told me. "I had to telephone her not to come. Daddy's feeling sick."

I was really disappointed. I practically made the stuffing all by myself.

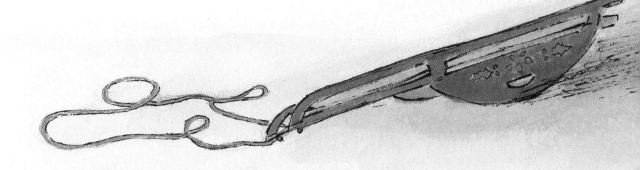

Daddy didn't look sick. He looked mad.

"Where'd you hide the beer?" he hollered at Mommy.

"You drank it all," she told him.

I guess he didn't believe her, because he started hunting for more. He looked everywhere, even in the grandfather clock. He was so mad I hid behind the couch and didn't move. Finally he went out.

It wasn't fair. He promised he'd take me sledding! I waited and waited.

Then I saw him coming back home. He had a
great big smile on his face. He'd remembered! I ran
outside with my sled.

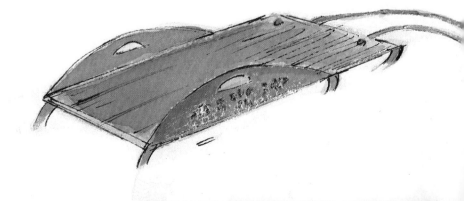

He tried to sit down on it, but he fell, plop, right in the snow. That made him mad all over again, and he threw the sled in the hedge, like it was *my* fault.

Mommy took him inside, and I heard yelling and screaming and glass falling.

I wished, just once, we could have a real Christmas like other people.

I wished, just once, we could have a real Christmas like other people.

After a while, Mommy remembered about me.
She was crying. "What shall we do with that huge
turkey?" she said. "Mrs. Field's not coming and
Daddy's too sick to eat."

"He's not sick," I told her. "He's drunk."

Mommy held me. "Daddy *is* sick, Lisa. He can't help his drinking. It makes him do hurtful, mean things he doesn't really want to do. The true, kind Daddy is the one who loves you so much he built you this beautiful sled."

"I wish the mean Daddy wouldn't always spoil Christmas," I said.

Mommy dried her eyes. "Well, this one doesn't have to be spoiled. *We* can't cure Daddy, so why don't we share our turkey with Mrs. Field, just as we planned."

"Let's take it to her house on my sled," I suggested.

I tied a bow on the turkey to make it look like a present, and we pulled it up the hill.
Mrs. Field was really surprised!

She lit the fire for us, and we counted the colors in the flames. Then I counted Mrs. Field's Christmas cards. She must know a lot of people.

"I drew a card for Daddy, and he didn't even open it," I told her. "I didn't do anything bad."

"No," she said. "And I know how sad and angry you must be. My own children felt that way once, when I used to drink too much. Only I'm okay now because I'm getting help. Your dad can, too, when he feels ready."

Mrs. Field touched my cheek. "But for now you can learn to be happier. You can try to do one of your favorite things every day."

I guess I was doing that already. I like turkey legs almost more than anything.

When we had to go, Mommy and I wrapped some turkey for Daddy. "Wait till I tell him what a great Christmas he missed," I said.

Mommy gave Mrs. Field a teary look. I hoped she wasn't going to cry again.

Then Mrs. Field gave me some silver bells. I tied them to my sled so we wouldn't get lost in the dark.

"Come back often," she said.

I told her I would. I felt safe at her house.

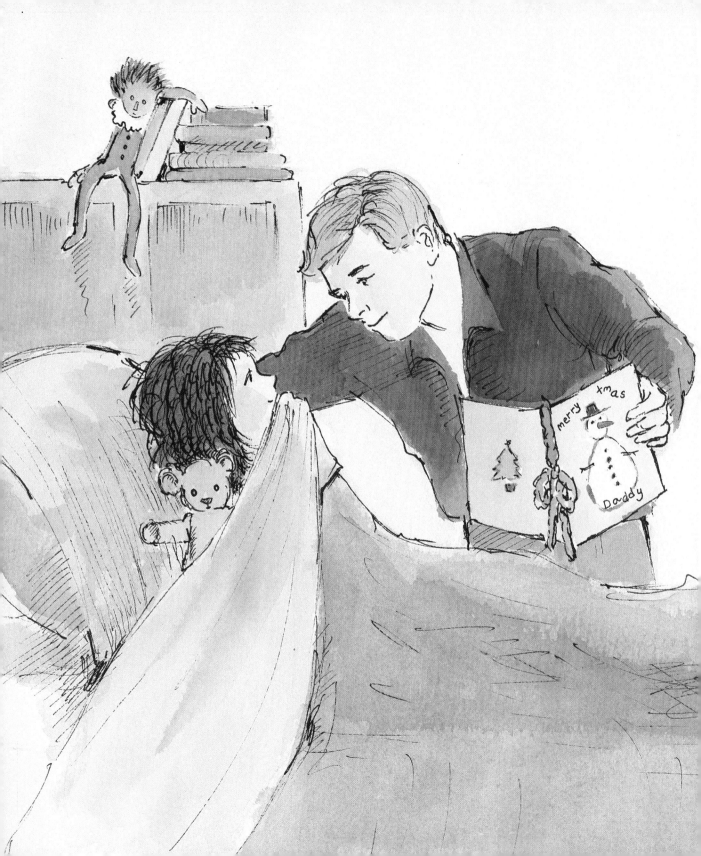

Daddy was asleep when we got home, but next morning he said, "Thank you for your card, sweetheart—I love it, and I love you, too! Sunday we'll go sledding, I promise."

I didn't really believe him about Sunday, but I guess it's okay. He said he loved me, and my sled is my best Christmas present ever.

I really hope Daddy takes me sledding on Sunday. But if he's sick again, I'll try not to mind.

If I take my sled to Mrs. Field's, and Mommy comes, too, I'll be doing my next most favorite thing.

A Note to Grown-ups

Alcoholism has been called the family disease. Anyone who has struggled with the drinking problem of a relative knows that sober family members, too, can suffer the helplessness and despair of alcoholism.

For children, having an alcoholic mother or father can be a double blow. Not only must they cope with the drinking parent; they often feel ignored by the sober parent who, understandably, may be overwhelmed by the problems of the drinker. The children tend to blame themselves and, without adequate support, may feel ashamed, confused, and alone. Because children of alcoholics are three to four times more likely than others to become alcoholics themselves, it is especially important to recognize and treat these emotional symptoms.

Parents and other caring adults can help by reassuring children that they are not responsible for the drinking. "We didn't cause the alcoholism, we can't control it, and we can't cure it." This message from Al-Anon, a program for adult family members, is equally apt for children, who also can learn to "detach with love" from the alcoholic behavior and focus on doing things that make them feel good about themselves. For more information about the Al-Anon organization, contact Al-Anon Family Group Headquarters, Inc., P.O. Box 862, Midtown Station, New York, N.Y. 10018 (212-302-7240).

Resources for individual help can be obtained from Children of Alcoholics Foundation, Inc., 200 Park Avenue, 31st Floor, New York, N.Y. 10166 (212-351-2680) or National Council on Alcoholism, 12 West 21st Street, New York, N.Y. 10010 (212-206-6770).

Judith Vigna